5-Minute
PUPPY TALES
⤛ for ⤜
Bedtime

Illustrated by Peter Stevenson

Derrydale Books
New York • Avenel

Editor: Joanne Hanks
Assistant Editor: Carey McIlvenny
Production: Christine Campbell

Illustrated by Peter Stevenson

Stories by Neil Arksey, Maria Buckingham, Paula Burgess,
Geoffrey Cowan, Selina Dowe, Nina Giglio, Suzanne Gilbakian,
Joanne Hanks, Timothy Harrison, Barbara Hayes, Wendy Hobson,
Kay Jones, Veronica Pennycook, Fran Pickering, Dorothea Ralli,
Marion Rose, Emily Smith, Malaika Rose Stanley, Sylvia Turtle,
Sandra Vigus, Brian Voakes, Anne Walker, Tim and Julie West,
Dennis Whelehan.

This 1996 edition published by Derrydale Books,
a division of Random House Value Publishing, Inc.,
40 Engelhard Avenue, Avenel, New Jersey 07001.

Random House
New York · Toronto · London · Sydney · Auckland

Printed in Hong Kong

A CIP catalog record for this book is available
from the Library of Congress.

ISBN 0-517-14241-4

8 7 6 5 4 3 2 1

There was nothing the three pups loved better than spending the day in an open boat, fishing, snoozing – or just listening to the sound of the waves lapping around them.

This day was different, something was wrong. Hector woke from a doze to find water slopping around the bottom of the boat. There, in the middle of the boat was a hole – and through it was flooding lots of very cold, very wet, very watery water.

"Help, help!" yelled Hector. "We're sinking!"

Quick as a flash, Horace jumped up and shoved Harold's umbrella handle down into the bottom of the boat, straight into the hole.

"Oh, my lovely umbrella!" wailed Harold. "It will break!"

But Horace wouldn't let go. . . While Hector rowed to the shore, Horace held Harold's umbrella handle firmly in the hole. Harold wasn't very happy by the time they reached the shore. But he had saved the day, and both his friends were very proud of him.

Harold's umbrella wasn't broken, only very wet. So the pups let it dry in the sun and then all went home for a celebration tea, in honor of Harold and his umbrella.

Chappy loved watching Puppy Television. Rhodda was his favorite dog presenter, he thought, as she rolled out sticky-backed plastic to make a kite. Chappy decided he would make a kite. He found some paper, glue, a roll of sticky tape and some string. He put newspaper on the floor and started.

Somehow it was not as easy as it looked. As he rolled out the paper the glue spread all over him and the paper stuck fast. The more he pulled, the worse mess he was in. The glue even stuck the lovely kite tail to his own tail. The roll of sticky tape caught on his foot and as he pulled at that, the tape twisted around him. When Mommy came in she could not see him for paper and tape.

"What's this sticky mess on the floor?" Chappy wagged his tail and the long string waved.

"Is that you Chappy?" she laughed. Chappy wagged again and Mommy unwound him. Next time, Mommy suggested, he should just watch Rhodda making it on television.

Daniel Basset loved tearing about the house like a mad thing. The house was very old and grand. It had large rooms and long corridors.

He looked forward to the day when he would be big enough to climb the stairs. He wanted to feel for himself the luxuriously soft bedroom carpets.

But for the time being he was quite content downstairs, with the polished wooden floors. Their shiny and slippery surfaces were just the greatest fun for sliding. All day long he skidded – nose down, face first – from room to room.

But Daniel hadn't quite got the hang of slowing down and stopping. And with his long floppy ears dangling over his eyes, steering could be a bit of a problem. He didn't mean to bump into things, it just happened that way.

Then one day, Daniel tried sliding sitting up. To his amazement, as he whizzed along he found his ears hung back. Now he could see where he was going!

He wouldn't have to bump into things any more.

And he didn't.

Much.

Ricky watched a TV film all about a space puppy who explored strange planets in a bone-shaped rocket.

"Wow! I wish I could do that!" thought Ricky.

Later, he asked Dad to help him make a rocket. They used some old cardboard boxes which Dad painted silver. At last, the rocket stood on the lawn, ready for take-off. Ricky climbed inside.

"Goodbye!" he said, pushing make-believe buttons.

"Wait!" called Mom, hurrying down the garden. "If you're space traveling, you'll need plenty to eat."

Mom gave Ricky some home-baked banana cookies. Ricky gobbled them up right away.

"I've made an apple pie ready for when you get home," smiled Mom, walking back towards the house.

"What would a real space puppy eat, Dad?" asked Ricky.

"Food in packets and tubes, I suppose," replied Dad.

"You mean, no home cooking?" said Ricky.

Dad shook his head so Ricky stepped out of the rocket.

"There's no place like Planet Earth!" he grinned, racing for the kitchen and apple pie . . . like a *rocket*!

BLODWYN'S ADVENTURE

One day, Blodwyn set out on an adventure.

"Stay inside the gate," barked Mom, "and don't get into any mischief!"

"As if I would!" thought Blodwyn, as she bounded down the garden path.

Blodwyn poked her fine bloodhound's nose into the air until she smelled something delicious.

She snuffled through the vegetable patch and sniffled past the roses. The smell led straight to the garden gate!

Blodwyn looked around. Mom was nowhere in sight, so she squeezed through the gap.

Outside, she ignored the rumbling traffic. She pressed her nose to the pavement and followed the trail.

Every now and then she looked up, and very soon she realized she was lost.

Blodwyn was frightened. She scampered about in panic until she caught another whiff of the delicious smell.

She sniffed back her tears and followed her nose. And when she looked up again, what a surprise! Her nose had led her home!

"Dinner's ready," barked Mom. "I bet you can smell that liver cooking miles away!"

Blodwyn didn't say anything. She just licked her lips and sighed with relief!

The local youth club was holding its annual track meeting in one week's time. The puppies gathered around the bulletin board were talking excitedly about the race. Only one stood back from the crowd, and he was kicking sadly at the floor.

"What's the matter, spindly legs, don't you want to lose another race?" yelled out one of the puppies and they all turned around to laugh at Zeppie.

"I know my legs *look* weak," thought Zeppie to himself, "but I'll show them." He ran home to get his training shoes on. For the next week Zeppie rose early and stayed up late running laps around his garden.

Finally race day arrived. Zeppie took his place at the starting line with the others. Ignoring their laughter, he bounded across the starting line as soon as the starting gun went off. When he reached the finish line he looked back to see the other puppies – still at the starting line coughing in the cloud of dust which had collected behind him!

Pete Pekinese was a pirate. He wore a patch over his eye, a cutlass at his side, and he sailed the seas looking for treasure!

One day he climbed the rigging to the look-out post. "Land ahoy!" he shouted to Bones Bernard, his mate. "And it could be a treasure island! Put her to starboard!"

"Aye, aye, Sir!" said Bones, steering the ship around. They landed at a little sandy cove.

"What now, sir?" said Bones, looking around.

"Now we explore, of course!" said Pete.

They crept up the beach, and there, beneath a spreading palm tree was . . . a casket. Could it be treasure?

Pete was just about to open it, when suddenly a girl appeared. "Paws off my jewel box, Pete!" she said. "And out of my room!"

"OK," said Pete forlornly. He knew when he was beaten.

Just on time Mom shouted, "Tea time," from downstairs. "Come and tell me what you want on your ships biscuits!"

Jojo the puppy hadn't grown into her ears and tail yet. They seemed too big for the rest of her. If she wasn't careful, she even stepped on them when she walked.

One night, Jojo couldn't sleep. She tossed and turned in bed instead.

"Mommy . . ." Jojo said.

"Yes, dear."

". . . I can't sleep."

"Why, dear?"

"My tail keeps flopping."

"*Who* is flopping?"

"OK – I am. But my tail keeps following me!"

"Try to lie still, dear."

"Mommy . . ."

"Yes, dear."

". . . I'm cold. And now my ears are flopping."

"Why don't you wrap your nice long ears around your neck? Then you'll be warm. You're lucky. You don't need a scarf," said Mom.

"OK," replied Jojo. And she was still . . . for a minute.

"Mommy . . . Teddy fell."

"If you wrap your tail around him, he won't fall," said Mom.

Jojo was so busy trying to keep her ears around her neck and her tail around her teddy, that she didn't toss and turn anymore. And she fell happily . . . quietly . . . asleep.

Freddie was, in most respects, a brave dog. He was frightened of nothing – except water. The very thought of getting into a big, deep pool made his hair stand on end.

But that was exactly what Freddie was going to have to do, because today was the first class trip to the swimming pool. "How can I get out of it?" he thought to himself. "Everyone will laugh at me when I can't swim!"

He was still wondering how to avoid getting wet when, at the pool, he saw a small figure splashing desperately in the water.

"Someone's drowning," he thought. Without thinking about himself he jumped in, paddled over to the drowning dog and helped him to the poolside.

"You are a brave dog, Freddie," said the teacher. "When did you learn that dogs can swim?"

Freddie just laughed.

If you are a small person, you know that sometimes you wish you were very tall. Well, it was the opposite with Gilbert Great Dane. You see Gilbert was a very big dog, who wished he was little! The only problem was, Gilbert wished so much to be little, that he forgot sometimes he was big.

For instance, Gilbert would swing on a tree branch, and the branch would break and Gilbert would land *bonk* on the ground. He was always trying on sweaters too small for him – and stretching them. And once he followed his best friend Kate Kitten through her cat door – only he got stuck and the Fire Department had to pull him out.

But although most of the time Gilbert imagined himself to be a little dog, he never forgot how lucky he was to be tall when he was in a crowd. At football games, or the Fourth of July fireworks display or the movies, Gilbert always had the best view.

om's favorite outing was the amusement park. He loved the feeling he had as the big wheel rose to the top. The loudest scream of delight always came from Tom as the rides twisted him down and round, round and down, faster and faster!

That special morning he woke early, bounced out of bed and rushed to the window. Oh no! Rain was pouring down, battering against the window in great heavy drops, racing down the pane in a hurry and a flurry. Tom looked out bleakly.

"Please can we still go today, Mom?" he begged. "If we get just one sunbeam, please can we go? Please!"

"Well," said Mom. "Since it is your favorite outing, if we do get one sunbeam by lunchtime, we can still go."

What a long morning it seemed. Tom played with his cars while the rain poured. He had a drink – the rain grew even heavier. Tom tried to draw but he kept looking out of the window – at more rain!

As lunchtime drew nearer, Tom had all but given up hope. Sadly he sat down at the table. As he did so, a bright shaft of sunlight broke out from behind the clouds; and the rain finally stopped. Tom could not believe his luck. Mom laughed.

"You must be the luckiest puppy in the world," she said. "Just one sunbeam all morning, and it came right on time!"

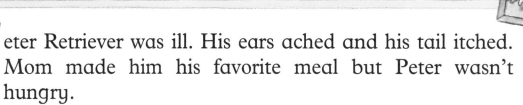

Peter Retriever was ill. His ears ached and his tail itched. Mom made him his favorite meal but Peter wasn't hungry.

Pandy came to see him.

"Shall I read to you, Peter?" she asked.

"No," said Peter. "I'm too ill."

Peter lay and looked at the picture on the wall opposite. It showed three puppies jumping around and having fun.

"I wish," said Peter, "that I could climb into the picture."

All at once the puppies in the picture started to move. They chased each other around faster and faster until one of them fell out onto Peter's bed and the others followed.

"Come and play," they said, so Peter jumped out of bed and raced off with them.

"Feeling better, dear?" said Mom coming in.

Peter opened his eyes. "Where have the other puppies gone?" he asked.

"You've been having a dream," said Mom.

Peter rubbed his eyes, "What a nice dream, I hope I have it again."

For the first time ever, Jamie was flying in an airplane. Sitting by the window, he felt the plane zoom down the runway and take off into the air. He watched carefully as the buildings grew smaller and smaller. "Look," he pointed, "there's a toy boat. And a toy train."

"Those are real boats and trains," Mom said. "They just look little because we're so high in the sky."

The plane finally landed an hour later, and it felt strange as it came down. Grandma was waiting for them as they left the plane. After they had all shared welcoming hugs and kisses, they hopped into Grandma's car and drove to a tall building. Taking the elevator up to Grandma's apartment felt strange too!

Inside the apartment, Jamie looked out of the huge balcony window. He saw a tiny boat far down. And tiny motor cars. And a tiny train. "We're on the airplane again!" he said.

Grandma laughed. "No Jamie. We're on the seventeenth floor. But fortunately we're not flying."

Sally Bloodhound and her family were staying with friends in a big old house in the countryside. Everyone had something to do except Sally, so she decided to explore. Nose to the floor, she followed a mysterious smell.

In her eagerness she forgot to watch where she was going and bumped into a flight of stairs with a *thonk*. She scampered up the stairs and discovered some attic rooms. Pushing open a door she peeped inside.

Sally was enchanted. Dolls and toys peeped from boxes and crates. A black trunk stood open with lacy dresses and beautiful velvet materials spilling out of it on to the floor. Underneath the window was a dusty old rocking horse, its paint faded and its tail thinned.

She poked about in the boxes, played with the toys and tried the clothes on. Tired out, she curled up in the armchair and went to sleep.

Downstairs it was dinner time – and no one could find Sally. "We'd better search the house," said father.

They all hurried away in different directions. But her cousin Billy knew where she would be. He ran off to his favorite room – and there she was. Still fast asleep in the chair.

Y ou're not a very good advertisement for health," said Scot. "You're much too overweight! I thought doctors were supposed to be healthy. Why don't you go on a diet?"

"I know, I know," said Dr. Bone. "But it's my job that makes me eat too much. You see, every day I start well: I get up early, have a very healthy breakfast, jog to work – then it all goes wrong!"

"Whatever do you mean?" asked Scot.

"Well, the first thing I see when I get in is my office door – with *DR. BONE* on it. That sets me thinking and my tummy rumbling. When my patients come in they greet me with, 'Hello, Dr. Bone.' That reminds me of my tummy some more. Then you can be sure that some-one needs an X-ray. Of course when I see it, I completely forget my diet and *have* to have a snack!"

"I don't understand!" said Scot. "What on earth is an X-ray?"

Have you ever had an X-ray? If so, you'll understand why it makes Dr. Bone feel so hungry!

Going to bed is fine when you are sleepy, but if you feel wide awake, bedtime can be boring.

One evening, Patrick Puppy did not feel tired at all.

"I want to stay up with you and Daddy," he said to his mother. "I want to watch grown-up television. I want to get out my train set. I want to play with my cars. I DON'T WANT TO GO TO BED!"

But up to bed Patrick had to go. As soon as Mommy Hauser had gone downstairs, Patrick started being naughty. He jumped up and down on the bed. He knocked the pillows onto the floor. He knocked the quilt off too. He screwed up the sheets and blankets. But at last he was so exhausted he fell asleep. His big brother, Jimmy, looked in and saw the mess. He tidied it up so that Patrick would not get into trouble.

"Has Patrick gone to sleep?" called Mommy.

"Asleep as good as gold," replied Jimmy.

Sometimes puppies have to have their little secrets.

Spot the puppy thought that he had a good memory. At bedtime he could remember what he had eaten for breakfast and what he had munched for dinner.

Of course, he could not remember much about what had happened last week or last month. As for when the grown-ups started talking about *last year*, well he did not understand that at all.

So all Spot could remember about trees was that they were always covered in leaves. When at the end of the summer, the leaves fell off the trees, Spot was AMAZED!

When Daddy said that the leaves fell off the trees for the cold winter and grew again in the warm summer, Spot said he thought trees were silly.

"I put on *warm* clothes in the cold weather and take them off in the *hot* weather," he yipped. "I've got more sense than trees have."

"You will understand when you are older," laughed Daddy.

It was a warm summer evening. Daisy sat in a chair on the patio, watching the sun go down. She sipped an ice-cool fruit drink. Suddenly, Daisy heard something by the garden shed.

"Who's there?" she called.

"Owwwwooo!" came the reply.

Daisy was so surprised, she spilled some of her drink on the patio table.

"Oh!" she cried.

"That doesn't sound much like a wolf!" said her brother Dave, stepping out from behind the shed. "I was pretending to be one. Did you like my howl?"

"It made me jump!" replied Daisy.

"Sorry!" said Dave. "I was only playing. Why don't you try howling?"

So Daisy howled as loudly as she could.

"Great!" shouted Dave. "May I sip your drink before I try again?"

Daisy handed over her plastic cup which was still half full.

"Watch out for the ice cubes," she said.

Too late – Dave had dropped the cup and some ice-cubes slipped down into his shirt.

"YEOOOOWWWW!" howled Dave, quickly pulling them out.

"That's *definitely* the best howl," smiled Daisy.

Bob was hiding behind a big shrub waiting for Timmy to find him. He peeped through a gap in the fence and there in the next garden was the smallest, fluffiest puppy he had ever seen. She had a blue bow on top of her head.

"Hello!" he shouted.

"Who are you?" said the tiny puppy.

"I'm Bob, what's your name?"

"Fifi."

"Come over and play hide-and-seek with us, Fifi."

"Mom doesn't like me to play with big dogs."

"We aren't big dogs, we're puppies too. Do you play games?"

"What are those?"

"We'll show you."

So Fifi squeezed through the fence and they explained the game to her.

"You can hide next, Fifi," said Timmy. So she did.

"Ready," she shouted, but they couldn't find her.

"She's gone home," said Bob.

"Yes, no – wait, what's that over there?" said Timmy. And there behind a big clump of yellow flowers, Fifi's little blue bow was sticking up.

Terry fought to find a way out of her bed. But her blankets would not give way. Whichever way she turned they wrapped themselves tighter and tighter around her short, stubby body. Finally, her tiny pink nose found a gap and she panted and gasped for fresh air.

She was desperate to get up early this morning. She didn't want to be late for the family picnic for the third year in a row. Her family had threatened to go without her if she wasn't on time. The sun had already crept through the curtains; it was getting late. She looked around her room groaning. She would never find her clothes under all this mess. The clock chimed dong, dong, dong. . . Eight o'clock! She stumbled out of the door, fell down the stairs and raced into the kitchen.

No one was there. They had gone without her.

Gloomily, she turned to go back upstairs and . . . bumped into her brother! "Terry, it's only seven o'clock. What are you doing up so early? You forgot to set your clock back last night, didn't you? Never mind, at least you're ready on time this year!"

Early one morning, the milkdog came to the door. Prudence Poodle liked the milkdog. She jumped up to lick his face, but she knocked over all the milk bottles.

"Woof! Woof!" barked Prudence.

"Too rough!" barked the milkdog.

"Bad dog!" barked Mom.

Later, the maildog came to the door. The maildog didn't like puppies. Prudence didn't like him either. She tried to bite his paws through the mailbox!

"Yap! Yap!" yelped Prudence.

"Don't snap!" yelped the maildog.

"Bad dog!" yelped Dad.

Next, the paperpuppy came to the door. Prudence tried very hard to be a good little puppy. She wagged her tail and the paperpuppy scratched her head.

Prudence didn't make a sound. She picked up the newspaper and carried it in her mouth. But when she reached the kitchen, the paper was chewed and soggy.

"Bad dog!" barked Mom.

"Bad dog!" yelped Dad.

That night, a robber came to the door. Prudence jumped up and bit his bottom.

"Bow-wow!" growled Prudence.

"Ow! Ow!" growled the robber.

"Good dog!" barked Mom.

"Good dog!" yelped Dad.

Hubert Husky hated having his hair cut. He had curly, fluffy hair that, when it grew long, stuck out, but he was very fond of it. Mrs. Husky always had a terrible time persuading him to go to the barber's, even though he looked much more handsome with short hair.

"You will feel much cooler," she would reason. Or she would try and coax him by promising sweets. Most of the time, however, she had to resort to practically dragging him down to the hairdresser's.

One day Hubert overheard his mother telling his father that it was time for Hubert to have his hair cut. Hubert ran out of the house and hid behind a neighbor's hedge. Mr. Spaniel came out into his garden and saw Hubert's hair sticking out from behind the hedge that Mr. Spaniel always kept perfectly neat and tidy.

In a flash, he reached for his garden shears and began chopping away at the hedge . . . or rather at Hubert. Poor Hubert was left short on the top and long on the sides!

He begged his mother to take him to the barber's to have it tidied up.

Misty and Cookie frolicked in the snow, their brown and white floppy ears hanging with icicles.

"Let's see if the ducks like this icy weather," called Misty. They ran to the pond where the water was solid and the ducks were sliding across it.

"Why are they standing on the water and not in it?" asked Cookie.

"I don't know," said Misty, "but it looks like fun." He gingerly stepped on to the pond. His legs spread in opposite directions and he slid on his tummy.

Cookie laughed and stepped onto the ice as well. She rolled on to her back and slid upside down into the ducks. They flew off squawking.

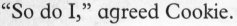

"You pups should learn to skate," said a large duck. He then gracefully spread his wings and skated across the pond. He brought back a willow branch, held in his beak.

"Hold on," and the pups grabbed it with their teeth. As the duck pulled them across the ice they squealed with joy.

"That was great!" said Misty, "I like skating."

"So do I," agreed Cookie.

Lucy Labrador had been invited to a costume party, but she had no idea what to wear. She sat down to watch television to see if that gave her any ideas.

On the screen she saw a commercial. A poodle was running around with a roll of toilet paper. "That gives me an idea!" Lucy exclaimed, and she rushed to the bathroom.

Grabbing a roll of toilet paper she wrapped herself up in it, and looked just like an Egyptian mummy!

She was the center of attention at the party, and won first prize in the costume competition.

But when she got home her parents were not very pleased. "You must ask us first, if you are going to take something," said her mother. "But I'm very pleased you won first prize."

Lucy promised she would ask them next time, and they put her trophy in pride of place on the mantelpiece.

Charlie was an Alsatian puppy who loved watching television. When Sally Corgi came round to visit she would ask, "Charlie, will you come and play hide-and-seek with me?" And Charlie would reply rather crossly, "Sally, can't you see I'm busy!"

It was the same when Percy Poodle came around to play. He would ask, "Hey Charlie, how about a game of football?" And Charlie would reply, "Not now Percy, I'm watching my favorite cartoon!"

His friends became really annoyed!

One day the television broke and Henry Bulldog took it away to be repaired. Poor Charlie was very upset!

When his friends came around to ask him to play, he reluctantly joined in. They played football and hide-and-seek, but the game Charlie enjoyed best was dressing up and acting out the parts of his favorite television characters.

After the television was fixed, Charlie decided it was much more fun to play with his friends than sit at home all day watching television.

Lucy was one of three Labrador puppies. Being the youngest and smallest she looked up to her elder brother and sister, Lionel and Laura.

Everything that Lionel and Laura did, Lucy wanted to do too. When they ate their supper, Lucy ate hers. When they sat down, Lucy sat down. And when they went to sleep, Lucy did too.

One day Lionel and Laura stood up in the bed that they all shared, and looking over the top of it started to wag their tails. Seeing her elder brother and sister do this Lucy tried to copy them, but she couldn't. She wasn't tall enough to see over the top of the bed. Try as she did she couldn't wag her tail. She looked at Lionel and Laura's tails wagging from side to side and then at her own but nothing happened.

Lucy got very upset. Not only could she not see what Lionel and Laura could over the top of the bed, but she couldn't wag her tail either.

Just as she was about to give up she saw her mother, carrying a present of a new, shiny red ball. Lucy yelped happily and it was then that she realized that her tail was wagging just as much as her brother's and sister's.

There was once a puppy who loved the rain. He loved jumping into puddles and sending water flying everywhere. One year it rained a lot and Splasher Puppy, as he was called, was happy. Then his boots started leaking.

"No more stamping in puddles until we can afford to buy new boots," said Mommy Dog, "and that won't be for a while."

In fact, Splasher Puppy had to wait until Christmas for new boots, and do you know, from the moment he got them, there was no more rain. Day after day was dry. Splasher became glummer and glummer.

Then one day when Grandpa was taking care of Splasher while Mommy and Daddy were out, he said he would make Splasher happy. Grandpa put Splasher into his boots. Then he set up the garden hose and sprayed masses of water over the lawn so that there were lots of puddles for Splasher to stamp in. Splasher was so happy. Then Grandpa cleared everything away before Mommy and Daddy got home. It had all been rather naughty, but lots of fun.

A fluffy, furry face, one black ear, one white ear and a little black button nose – that was Daisy May, the happiest, bounciest puppy in the world.

"Daisy May," called her cat friend Saffron. "Where are you?"

The door flew open, and in rushed Daisy May. "Please help me put holly on top of my grandfather's picture," Saffron said. "It's too high for me."

Daisy May stretched and stretched but could not reach the top.

"Oh dear!" cried Saffron.

"Don't worry," said Daisy May. "If I stand still, you can jump on my back and I'm sure you could reach."

Up she jumped and *yesssss* she reached the top. Daisy May *was* excited. She wagged her tail hard, but hadn't seen the pile of holly on the floor, "Uh oh, something has gotten my tail!" she cried. Why was Saffron laughing so much? Stuck on the end of her tail was a prickly piece of holly. "Come here," said Saffron giggling, "You helped me, now I'll help you," and she tugged the holly from Daisy May's tail.

T he suspect is at least six foot tall," said Sherlock Hound. The famous detective had just examined the giant pawprints that led from Mr. and Mrs. St. Bernard's kitchen. "Judging by the size of those prints and the amount of food missing, we have a giant robber with a king size appetite! If we wait up, he's bound to be back tonight."

Sure enough, that night as Sherlock Hound lay in wait with three burly detectives, they heard the sound of heavy feet padding across the kitchen floor.

"Get, ready. . . NOW!" said Sherlock, and the four detectives leapt on the villain.

Oh dear. What a mistake. The villain wasn't six foot tall. He wasn't even a villain. He was Bertie – Mr. and Mrs. St. Bernard's son.

"I was feeling hungry. I just crept down for a midnight snack," he exclaimed sheepishly.

Next time you see a St. Bernard puppy, take a look at its' large feet. You'll see why Sherlock Hound made such a silly mistake.

31

N ew neighbors," yelped Ali, wagging her tail furiously, as the bright yellow moving truck came to a stop outside the house next door. She had watched the empty house for two weeks hoping for a playmate to race through the park with her woof-ball. Finally she could contain herself no longer and jumping off her window stool she ran downstairs.

As she flung the door open two floppy ears, a long nose and a sad little face peered down from the truck. Ali scampered up and introduced herself, "Hello, my name is Ali, would you like to come and play chase with me?"

But the little puppy just disappeared back into the truck without a word. Ali hung her head, and turned to go home. As she got to the front door she heard a little yelp behind her call, "Don't go!"

Ali looked up at her new neighbor who said, "I'm sorry if I was rude but you were so friendly – you frightened me, let's start again shall we?" Ali practically knocked herself out wagging her tail in agreement.

Jimbo Jack Russell stared once again at the big map of the world he had on his wall and sighed.

"Wouldn't it be just wonderful to visit one of these places?" he thought. But airplane tickets cost so much money these days, and boat tickets weren't much cheaper either.

How could Jimbo *ever* afford to buy one?

Suddenly Jimbo had an idea.

"I don't need to buy a ticket to go on vacation. All I need is a stamp!" And with that he climbed into a dog shaped envelope and hopped down to the post office.

Unfortunately poor Jimbo could only afford a second class stamp, and it was a week before he arrived.

Bernard St. Bernard loved sledding, and he couldn't wait for the winter's snow to fall.

One morning when he looked out of the window, all the world was white. He dressed quickly, and got his sled out of the garden shed. Dragging it to the top of a big hill, he climbed on and pushed off.

"Wheeeeeeeeeeeee!" he yelled, as he whizzed and whooshed down the slope. "Whoopee!" he whooped, as the sled slipped, slid and slithered across the snow. "Yippee!" he yelped, as he zoomed and zipped past other puppies on their sleds. "Oh dear, oh dear!" he cried, as he zipped, zoomed, slithered, slid, slipped, whooshed and whizzed straight into a large snowdrift!

Luckily, Bernard's father had seen the whole thing, and he rushed over to dig Bernard out, and give him a hot drink.

"That was fun," said Bernard, when his teeth had stopped chattering. "I think I'll do it again. But this time I don't think I'll start from quite so high up!"

After a fun afternoon playing puddles, Priscilla pup stood glumly on the living room rug, scrubbed white and fluffy, a pink bow tied neatly between her ears. Mrs. Poodle liked ribbons and even her pet goldfish wore them!

"You look absolutely adorable, Priss!" said Mrs. Poodle, going to answer the door. "My friend, Mrs. Rover will go absolutely soppy over you."

Priscilla cringed. Mrs. Rover meant cuddles . . . lipstick . . . and perfume. Yuk! She may be a puppy, but she was no sissy.

And there she was – Mrs. Rover – crouching, grinning, in the doorway. It was now or never. Yapping excitedly, Priscilla galloped towards the waiting arms.

"Ahh, woochie, coochie, poochie, poosey, woosey! How's my precious . . . ?"

But Priscilla kept on going – past Mrs. Rover – right off the doorstep and *sploosh* – into the deepest, muddiest puddle.

"Uh-oh-ooh-ahhhh-eeeargh!" gasped Mrs. Rover, suddenly dashing to the living room, as wet Priscilla headed back indoors.

Priscilla shook her fur and wagged her tail. Things hadn't turned out so bad after all!

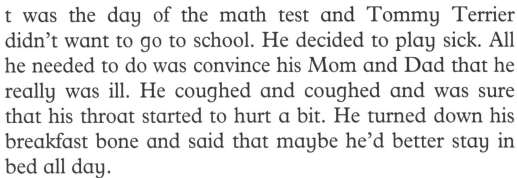

It was the day of the math test and Tommy Terrier didn't want to go to school. He decided to play sick. All he needed to do was convince his Mom and Dad that he really was ill. He coughed and coughed and was sure that his throat started to hurt a bit. He turned down his breakfast bone and said that maybe he'd better stay in bed all day.

The problem was that a couple of days earlier, Mrs. Terrier had met Tommy's teacher and so she knew all about the math test.

Tommy was wrapped up comfortably in bed when his parents came upstairs and stood outside his bedroom door. Mr. Terrier said loudly that Tommy could come with him to his grocery shop. He'd be useful wrapping up customers' packages and stacking the shelves. But Mrs. Terrier thought Tommy would be better coming into her office, because she had lots of sorting papers and filing he could help with. Mr. Terrier said Tommy could add up all that day's deliveries and see that none were missing. Mrs. Terrier replied that she had long lists of sums to be checked and change to be counted out.

Their conversation stopped as Tommy came running out of his bedroom, pulling on his school uniform and grabbing his books. "The math test doesn't sound so bad after all!" he thought.

At home, Judy copied her mother's circus dog tricks. She easily did flips and jumps and paw stands. But at the yoga class she floundered about on all fours, trying to stretch up and across or out and over. Everyone else could do it, but not Judy.

The teacher barked, "Just lift your left front paw over your nose and turn your right back paw to the left and slide your left back paw more to the right and then center yourself."

Judy tried, but the teacher said, "It's no use. You're uncoordinated."

Then the teacher told them to do a headstand.

All the students kept falling over. But not Judy. She stood on her head like an expert.

"If you can do this," the teacher said, "why can't you do the other poses?"

Judy said, "I don't know my left from my right."

The teacher laughed. Then she tied big Ls and Rs to Judy's paws. After this she was the best yoga student.

One bright morning, Tim ran into his back garden as usual. He loved an early race around the flowers and bushes. But today there was an unknown smell in the air. Tim froze and looked around.

"Good morning!" murmured a slow voice above him. He looked up and saw in the branches of his tree a sleek, smug, Siamese cat.

Tim was annoyed. What was this stranger doing in his territory? He leapt up barking as fiercely as he could.

"Such a fuss so early in the morning!" she purred lazily, before drawing herself up, stretching gracefully, and settling down for a gentle doze. This wouldn't do. He would show this newcomer who was boss.

Tim marched around and around the base of the tree, trying to figure out a plan. After a lot of time wasted and no ideas at all, Tim was upset. "This is no good," he thought. "I'll get on with the gardening as usual and ignore her."

The sun was beating down by now, so Tim set up the sprinkler to water the lawn. Suddenly there was a terrific yowl, "**yiaouwww**!" And an angry, sodden Siamese leapt into the air before bounding back over the fence into her garden.

Tim chuckled over his "mistake" all afternoon. "I showed that stuck-up cat!" he muttered to himself.

The weather was too cold and too wet. Sam did not want to go out to play. Then one morning his poodle friends, Laura and Billy called.

"Come on out and play in the snow," they said. Sam looked out and the ground was white, the trees were white, and the grass had disappeared.

"Where has the grass gone?" asked Sam, very puzzled.

"Silly! It's under the snow. You can go out but keep warm," said his mother as she wrapped him up in a scarf, coat, and hat. Sam ran out. The snow was cold and wet.

"Ugh! It's all wet!" he grumbled, as he stepped carefully along the path. From behind Laura pushed him and he slid down a slope to the bottom. Curious, he pushed his nose through the snow and it stuck on his face. Then he tried to eat it but gave up because it did not taste of anything.

"What's it for?" Sam asked puzzled.

"This," said Laura and threw a snowball straight at him.

"Take that!" laughed Sam, as he threw one back. Then they played happily in the snow until it was time for lunch.

Have you ever wondered what happens to the world when you close your eyes? Does it stay where it is, or does it disappear when your eyes are shut? This was what Willy Whippet was wondering as he lay in bed unable to sleep.

"What if, when I open my eyes again, everything is gone?"

Poor Willy was very tired but was too afraid to close his eyes. "Now then young Willy," said his dad, "don't be so afraid. I'll prove to you that the world stays right where it is when you close your eyes."

Mr. Whippet got Willy first to close one eye on its own then the next, so that he could always see the world out of one.

"It's exactly the same when both your eyes are shut," said his Dad.

Now Willy is never scared to close his eyes at night. But occasionally, you might just catch him squinting and winking – just to make sure.

Mommy Dachshund frowned.

"Don't eat so fast, Jinna! The other puppies have only just started their breakfast and you've already finished yours. No, you may NOT eat their food too! You can get down."

So Jinna scampered off into the garden, looking for mischief. She found some raspberry bushes growing low down, so she tasted them.

"Oh, yummy!" she exclaimed.

Presently her mother came out to pick a bowlful of them for lunch.

"Goodness," she exclaimed, "that's odd! There isn't a single berry left except on the very top branches."

And then she saw Jinna.

Jinna usually looked like a tiny brown silky sausage, with very short legs and big sploshy feet. But now her tummy was puffed out like a shiny brown balloon, and she could hardly waddle. Her little legs were quite hidden by her tummy and only her sploshy feet showed.

"Oh, you naughty puppy," her mommy laughed. "You certainly haven't got room for any lunch! I hope you won't be sick!"

Jinna thought about it and decided it had been worth it.

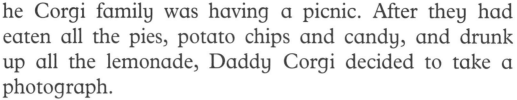

The Corgi family was having a picnic. After they had eaten all the pies, potato chips and candy, and drunk up all the lemonade, Daddy Corgi decided to take a photograph.

"It will look lovely in the family album," said Daddy Corgi.

But the little Corgi puppies wouldn't sit still. Charlie Corgi was the youngest, and he was the worst of all.

"Keep still, Charlie," said his Daddy, "or I won't be able to take your picture."

So Charlie did as he was told.

But at that moment a wasp appeared. He came buzzing around because he saw lots of crumbs. Daddy Corgi tried to chase him away, but he landed on Daddy's nose.

Charlie grabbed the camera.

"Keep still, or I won't be able to take your picture," he said.

Daddy Corgi ran away, trying to shake the wasp off his nose. All the puppies laughed and cheered, while Charlie took a photograph.

"It will look lovely in the family album," said Charlie.

Jasper and Jimmy were the two unlikeliest friends, but they stuck together through thick and thin – which is exactly what they were. Jimmy was small and tubby, Jasper was tall and thin.

Around the neighborhood they were known as the "Two Js," and anyone who knew them crossed the road to avoid the pranksters.

One Saturday the twosome strolled into town looking for trouble. Barnabus, a newcomer, was exploring the town. Unknown to him the "Js" were preparing to sneak up behind him, ready to throw bags of flour at him.

As he was pausing to look into the fountain, Barnabus noticed the tricksters' reflection in the water and neatly side-stepped their charge.

The two puppies emerged covered head to toe in sticky, gloopy, gluey dough and dragged themselves home very slowly. Meanwhile Barnabus received welcoming handshakes and some applause too!

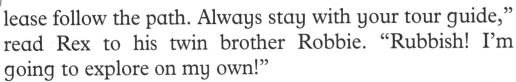

Please follow the path. Always stay with your tour guide," read Rex to his twin brother Robbie. "Rubbish! I'm going to explore on my own!"

"But they say that Barking Mansion is haunted! The ghost of Sir Woofalot walks the corridors," said Robbie. "I'm staying on the path."

But Rex was a nosey puppy. When he wanted to explore, nothing could stop him. Rex hadn't gone far when he began to have second thoughts.

"Oh my word!" he thought. "Someone, or something is watching me! What was that strange rattling noise? It sounded like chains! Did the eyes in that painting move? What about that suit of armor – I'm sure it started to move!"

Rex had had enough. Back he ran, as fast as his legs would carry him, to join the tour group.

"You look as if you've seen a ghost!" said Robbie.

"Sir Woofalot himself!" panted Rex. "Next time, I'm going to stay on the path!"

Billy Bulldog hated bathtime. He didn't like the water. He didn't like the soap, and worst of all was when Mommy used the shampoo!

Mommy bought Billy a rubber duck, but Billy still didn't like baths. Mommy bought him a toy boat, but he still didn't like baths. She even bought him a diving dog, but that didn't make him like bathtime either. Mommy just didn't know what to do!

One day Mommy had a brilliant idea. She went to the bathroom and ran Billy's bath, and she put in lots of bubble bath, then she cried out. "Help! Help! The soap monster is here!"

Billy rushed to the bathroom to rescue his Mommy. He dived into the bath and began popping all the bubbles. When he had finished he saw Mommy smiling at him. "You really are a brave little puppy!" she said. "And wasn't that fun!"

Billy had to admit it had been great fun.

"But next time you rescue me from the soap monster," said Mommy. "I think you'd better take your clothes off first!"

It was autumn time and Merry Maddie Labrador was sitting beneath a horse chestnut tree in her garden. It was a tall tree, with beautiful curly branches and leaves grouped together like fat green fingers on a huge green hand. Lately however the green leaves seemed to have turned brown.

Merry Maddie, very fond of her big tree, worried that it was ill. Suddenly one of the brown leaves fluttered down past Maddie's nose and landed on the ground.

"Oh my goodness!" squealed Maddie. "My poor tree is falling apart!" Maddie tried in desperation to glue the leaves back on, but to no avail. Over the next few weeks all the leaves fell off and the tree was left completely bare.

Poor Maddie sobbed and sobbed.

"What's wrong?" said a passing friend.

"I'm such a rotten gardener," said Maddie. "All the leaves have fallen off my tree."

"Don't worry," said her friend, "that's just autumn. Lots of trees lose their leaves at this time of year. They'll grow back in spring."

And do you know? They did.

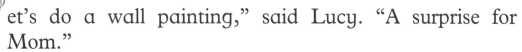

Let's do a wall painting," said Lucy. "A surprise for Mom."

Her brothers, Collie and Dobie, each carried a can between their teeth. But little Popsie puppy could only manage a brush. Their tails all wagged excitedly. "The brushes are small," warned Lucy, "so we'll have to work fast." Dipping one in blue, she began painting the sky.

Using his big swishing tail dipped in brown, Collie painted a tree.

Dobie was tall so, with a brush in his mouth, he stretched up to paint a yellow sun.

But Popsie, standing on a box to dip her brush in the green paint, lost her balance and fell into the pot. **Plosh**!

Pulling Popsie out, Lucy wiped her sister across the wall. "Hey! Popsie makes a great brush!" she said. "Painting grass is easy now."

Just then, the door opened and Lucy's mother stood there staring. "*My lovely wall!*" she shrieked in horror.

Lucy dropped Popsie. Popsie scampered for cover.

"*My . . . beautiful . . . carpet . . . !*" gasped Lucy's mother, watching the lengthening trail of green paw prints.

After that she had no choice but to choose green as the living room color.

Azeem ambled down the path which led into the forest. He was bored again and looking for some light entertainment, which usually meant chasing squirrels.

It had been raining the night before, so he gingerly picked his way around the puddles. Out of the corner of his eye he saw Cyril Squirrel dart up a tree. Growling menacingly, he bounded after him. Just then, Irene Squirrel came running down a huge oak tree so Azeem turned quickly to chase after her. From out of nowhere Sam Squirrel went scampering right in front of his nose, and Azeem changed direction again.

"I'll definitely catch up with Sam," Azeem gleefully thought to himself. But Sam had other ideas. . .

Suddenly Azeem found himself skidding across the field, his legs furiously waving in the air. He had been so busy chasing Sam that he didn't notice the puddle which the squirrel had so elegantly jumped over.

"Serves you right," laughed the squirrels from the branches up above as a bedraggled Azeem limped home.

Kevin had a computer. "It can do almost anything!" he told his friends Ben and Marty.

"Can it draw?" asked Marty.

"Watch!" replied Kevin.

He used it to make Marty's face appear on the screen. Then Kevin pressed a button on the keyboard to print the picture.

"My computer can remember, print anything I want and even spell words!" said Kevin.

"Let's use it to produce our own puppy comic," suggested Ben.

Kevin, Ben and Marty set to work with the computer, writing, designing and printing page after page. If they made a mistake, they just threw the page on the floor and started again. Soon there was paper everywhere!

Their comic was a big success. "Great! Thanks!" said all their friends who were each given a copy.

"Thank Kevin's computer!" said Ben and Marty.

"It can do anything," repeated Kevin, proudly.

"In that case it can tidy up your room," said his mom who had just seen the mess.

Of course, the computer couldn't. Kevin, Ben and Marty had to do that on their own.

It was a fine, dry winter's day and the puppies had arranged to meet on the village green for a game of soccer. Grandpa Jack Russell had agreed to sit on a bench and watch so that no harm came to anyone and everything seemed set for a good afternoon.

However, there was a little problem because Yipper Russell had brought his ball, his brother Yapper had brought his ball and their friend Flop Ears Bloodhound had also brought his ball. They all wanted their soccer balls to be used. For a while there was quite an argument.

Then Grandpa Jack Russell called out from the bench, "Why don't you use all three balls? Three times the number of you little fellows will be able to kick a ball at a time. The game will be three times faster and most likely three times as much fun."

"Why not?" thought the puppies.

They chose three goalies and played with the three balls. And they had MOUNTAINS of fun.

"When friends play together, rules can be rearranged a little," said Grandpa.

Michael Mastiff was afraid of the dark. He hated going to bed. Mommy always left the hall light on so Michael wouldn't be frightened.

One night as Mommy was tucking Michael in he asked. "Why don't I like the dark?"

"What do you think of when the lights go out?" asked Mommy.

"I think there's something hiding under the bed."

Mommy looked under the bed. "There's nothing there," she said. "Why don't you try to think of nice things, like Santa Paws, or the Easter Bulldog, or all the presents you'll get for your birthday?"

"I'll try," promised Michael, and he shut his eyes.

That night Michael had a lovely dream all about the nice things he did. Playing in the park with his dad, playing soccer with his friends, and all the wonderful things he got at Christmas.

He was never afraid of the dark ever again!

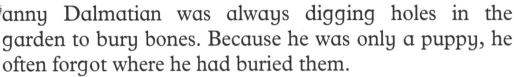

Danny Dalmatian was always digging holes in the garden to bury bones. Because he was only a puppy, he often forgot where he had buried them.

"I wish Danny Dalmatian had a better memory," said his aunt. "He is ruining my garden with all his digging."

Then she thought that she could save herself some work. She gave Danny a part of the garden all to himself.

"You can dig as many holes here as you like."

Danny Dalmatian was delighted. All through the winter he buried bones, and then dug lots of holes trying to find them again. He had a wonderful time.

When it was spring, Aunt Dalmatian planted vegetables in that part of the garden that Danny had dug up for her. The soil was already nice and soft, so she didn't have to go to the trouble of digging it.

"Thank you, Danny," said Aunt Dalmatian, and gave him a big, juicy bone.

But she didn't let him bury it in her vegetable garden!

I love the snow!" said Harold the Husky pup. "The colder, the better!"

He was staying with his cousin Penny.

"It's always cold at home," Harold explained. "I don't mind it a bit!"

"Well, it isn't here," said Penny. "You were lucky we had a snowstorm last night."

Harold and Penny built a snowpup in the garden, then threw snowballs at a tree trunk.

"I'm getting cold," said Penny, although she was well wrapped up. "Come indoors and Dad will make us both a hot chocolate drink!"

"I'll be along soon," called Harold. "Like I said, I don't mind it being cold!"

As Penny sipped her drink, dad made another one for Harold who played and played in the snow.

"I was enjoying myself so much, I forgot all about my drink!" said Harold when he finally came in.

Harold took one sip and pulled a funny face. "Ooh! It's cold!" he groaned.

"I thought that's the way you liked it!" teased Penny as her dad warmed the drink again.

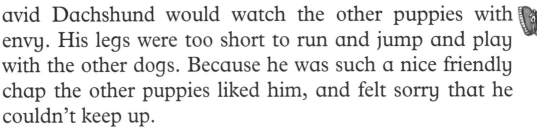

David Dachshund would watch the other puppies with envy. His legs were too short to run and jump and play with the other dogs. Because he was such a nice friendly chap the other puppies liked him, and felt sorry that he couldn't keep up.

One day, as David was watching his friends play and jump and run, Gary Greyhound dashed over to the Dachshund pup. "I've got a surprise for you," panted Gary. "Follow me," and off he rushed.

David followed with a waddling trot, and was soon quite out of breath. When he caught up with Gary quite a crowd had gathered. "Look what we've got for you," announced Gary.

The crowd parted, and there was a shiny new skateboard! "We all chipped in a bit of our pocket money," said Gary. "But it was my idea."

David was so happy he didn't know what to say! So now, while the other puppies jump and run and play, David can keep up by whizzing along on his skateboard.

You are a mucky puppy," said Benjy's mom. "You've got a mucky face, mucky paws, mucky ears – just about mucky everything. Next time you come home like this you're going straight in the bath for a scrubbing like you've never had before!"

Well, Benjy didn't have long to wait. Next day, when he got home after a hard day's play, his mother took one look at him and ordered him straight upstairs to the bath.

Well, she soaped and she shampooed and she rubbed and she scrubbed and she rinsed until Benjy was so clean he sparkled.

Benjy took one look at himself in the mirror and liked what he saw. "Mom, I think I prefer being clean," he said. "I'm never going to get dirty again."

And do you know, Benjy never came home dirty again . . . well, hardly ever.

Bye, bye Millie," said Millie's mom, giving Millie a wave with her bushy tail and trotting off to work. Millie stood forlornly at the barnyard gate and watched her run far away over the fields.

Millie was miserable. "I want my mom," she howled.

"Hey, Millie, what's wrong?" said Cocky Cockerel. "Lost your waggy tail?"

Millie looked behind her and yelped in horror. Cocky was right. Her tail had gone!

Millie searched the pig sty. But her tail wasn't there.

Millie combed the cow shed. But her tail wasn't there.

"How could I be so careless?" Millie moaned. Just when she had given up all hope, she heard a bark.

And there was her mom coming back across the field. Millie had never been so pleased to see anyone in her life.

"Hello!" said her mom. "I could see you waving for miles!"

And when Millie looked round, what do you think she saw?

Her very own waggy tail!

Tiger the little West Highland Terrier loved cookies. It didn't matter what kind, he loved them all. He dedicated every waking moment of his life to eating as many as possible.

"If you eat any more cookies," his mother would say. "You'll turn into one!"

Now Tiger was quite a lazy dog and when he wasn't eating cookies he would generally be sleeping.

One day when Tiger was asleep he had a very strange dream. He had eaten rather too many cookies and was feeling full up when all of a sudden, he had a funny sensation in one of his paws. It felt sort of crispy. No, that's not quite right, more sort of crumbly. To his horror, Tiger's whole body began to change.

"Tiger!" exclaimed his Aunt Joyce. "You've turned into a dog shaped cookie!"

"Thank goodness it was only a dream!" thought Tiger, when he awoke. But it's funny, he never did eat quite so many cookies after that.

Ned Newfoundland took great pride in his looks and swaggered through town with his nose in the air. "I'm too good for this town," he boasted to his friends, as he flicked his hair back and flashed his gleaming white teeth.

Before Christmas, his mother organized a day trip to the city, which made Ned smirk happily. When they arrived he looked around thinking, "The city is so sophisticated – just like me."

No sooner had he said this than a taxi drove through a huge muddy puddle, drenching him. "Oh no, my tartan coat!" he yelped. Not a good start to the trip.

By the end of the day, Ned was exhausted and angry. He had been soaked and trodden on, and had gotten lost in a big department store – twice.

"I'm too glamorous for the city," Ned muttered to his friends, "I'm sticking to town life," and he strutted off down the road.

Just then a taxi zoomed by and seconds later Ned was heard yelling, "Oh no!" as he stood dripping with muddy water from head to toe.

Tina Skye Terrier was tiny. Everyone teased her because she was the smallest in the class. She pretended she didn't mind but it made her very unhappy.

One day there was quite a commotion in the village square. "What's happening?" asked Tina.

"One of the Rabbit children has fallen into a hole," someone said, "and the opening is too small for anyone to reach him."

"Perhaps I could reach him," said Tina. "I'm very small."

The crowd turned to look at her.

"Oh, please," said Mrs. Rabbit, in tears, "would you try?"

They all trooped along the road and across a field to where the Rabbit children waited by a narrow slit in the ground.

"Hold my legs," said Tina and wriggled herself through the opening. She reached down and just managed to grab hold of the little rabbit at the bottom of the hole. "Pull!" she called. They pulled and up came Tina and the young rabbit, rather dirty and frightened, but none the worse for his adventure.

After that, no one ever teased Tina about being small.

Mommy I don't feel well," said Sam. "My tummy hurts."

It was the first day of school, and Mrs. Ruff couldn't help thinking that Sam was really all right. He just didn't want to go!

"Would you like some breakfast?" she asked. "Oh yes please," said Sam. "Oh, eh . . . no, I'm not hungry," he finished, looking longingly at the breakfast table.

"In that case, I think we had better pay a visit to Dr. Dawg. He'll soon make you better."

Now Sam had been to Dr. Dawg's before, and Dr. Dawg meant just one thing – nasty medicine! And nasty medicine was not what Sam's tummy needed right now.

"You know, I'm feeling better already. I'll just have a bit of breakfast and I'll be off to school," said Sam.

Sam's mother said nothing and passed the toast.

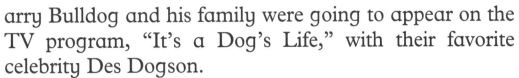

Barry Bulldog and his family were going to appear on the TV program, "It's a Dog's Life," with their favorite celebrity Des Dogson.

Barry and his mother and father had chosen to answer the questions on trees – their specialty. But, because he was so nervous, Barry had forgotten almost all he could remember. "Where does an acorn come from?" he asked his dad. "I can't remember if it's the ash, the oak or the beech tree."

"It's the oak," said Mr. Bulldog. "But I don't think they'll ask anything that simple."

They were led onto the stage, and the show started. The Bulldog family beat all the other contestants, and only had one question to answer for the big prize – a complete collection of Lassie videos, and Barry had to answer it. He was so nervous!

"Boy, you look edgy," joked Des Dogson. "You look like someone chewing a wasp! Here's your question for the big prize. From what tree does the acorn come?"

"Oh, I know that!" exclaimed Barry with relief. "It's the oak!"

"That's correct! You've won!" said Des Dogson.

Well, it was a good thing Barry wanted to check his facts.

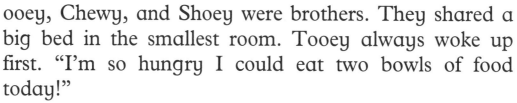

Tooey, Chewy, and Shoey were brothers. They shared a big bed in the smallest room. Tooey always woke up first. "I'm so hungry I could eat two bowls of food today!"

"You always want two bowls of food, Tooey. I'm hungry, too," said sleepy Chewy, as he began to chew the edge of their blanket.

"Stop that, Chewy! You can't eat our blanket. Keep that up and we will have nothing left to sleep under!" cried Tooey. "You always have to chew on everything."

"I know what I would like," yawned little Shoey, as he climbed out of the basket, "a nice big, fluffy slipper to chew on."

"Slippers and shoes aren't food, Shoey," said Tooey, following his little puppy brother into the bedroom closet. "If slippers were food our parents would walk around with fluffy slippers in their mouths, instead of on their paws!"

This made all the puppies laugh so hard they were soon rolling on the floor. They were so busy playing they did not even notice the four breakfast dishes which had been laid out on the table. One for Chewy, one for Shoey and two for Tooey!

r. Beefy Bernard, the drama teacher, was organizing the school pantomime – again. He was a big dog who bullied his puppies into playing small parts but kept the lead for himself. This normally meant that he got to leap about and throw cream bones at the others.

The night of the pantomime arrived and Mr. Beefy hogged the stage. The puppies could barely bark their lines out. Backstage they growled, "If he throws one more cream bone at us we're leaving the stage."

Finally the last act arrived and Mr. Beefy had just reached his final flourish when he disappeared . . . and then reappeared . . . and disappeared.

Mr. Beefy had fallen down a *mysteriously* open trap-door onto a trampoline and there was no way of stopping him.

The next year Mr. Beefy was reluctant to direct the pantomime – and even refused to play a part!

Floppy tossed and turned on his pillow. He couldn't sleep. He tried counting bones, but it made his tummy rumble. Things kept popping into his head – like the fact that he had not learned his spelling for school tomorrow! Oh dear! And he had promised his mom he would try to spell them *all* right. Quietly, he turned on the light and read the words on the paper by his bed.

Gradually the words started to float before his eyes: "brother, mother, hither, thither, where, there, why, when . . ." Then they all began to sprout legs and arms. They reached out to join hands and began to dance around in a circle. Higgledly, piggledly, in and out, around and around they pranced like a country dance. Then they started to slow down. They moved back into the right order again and lay down to sleep.

Strangely, Floppy did not feel tired the next morning. He decided to "forget" to mention that he had not practiced his spelling.

But Mom did not forget for long, and as soon as he arrived home she asked how he had done.

"I got them all right!" said Floppy proudly. "It was as easy as dreaming!"

Poor Scamp was miserable. His famous uncle, the Great Linguini, was in town with the circus and Scamp was stuck in bed with a bad cold.

Scamp sipped his nasty lemon drink and pushed his book off the bed. He'd read it at least five times. He had never been so bored in all his life. If only he could get better and see his uncle doing back flips and somersaults at the circus.

Just then the doorbell rang. Scamp pricked up his ears and heard his dad cry, "I don't believe it!" Scamp ran down the stairs quickly to see what was going on.

When he arrived at the front door he couldn't believe his eyes. Right in the middle of the street was Uncle Linguini with the whole circus lined up behind him. There were elephants playing trumpets, laughing hyenas, monkeys dressed as clowns, and best of all, Uncle Linguini riding an incredible unicycle.

"Hi Scamp. Hope you're feeling better," said Uncle Linguini. Scamp felt great.

Simon felt nervous. He had been to the dentist lots of times with his big sister. In fact, the door of her closet was covered in stickers from the dentist! Somehow, though, it was different going for your first time. What would it be like? Simon took a deep breath and walked into the office.

"Hello, young fellow-me-lad," said Dr. Barker. "Hold that for me, there's a good chap," and he gave Simon a tiny mirror. "Just take a look in here, will you?" he said. "I seem to have something stuck in my teeth," and with that he sat in his own chair and opened his mouth wide. Simon looked in.

"All I can see are shiny white teeth," he said.

"Good job," said the dentist. "Sit in my place and let's see if yours are as shiny. Would you like a ride?" He pressed a lever and Simon's seat rose then came down again. As Simon laughed, Dr. Barker took a look in his mouth.

"Nothing wrong with those," he said. "Will you come back again to look at my teeth?"

"Yes, please," said Simon proudly. On that day, he decided he would like to be a dentist when he grew up.

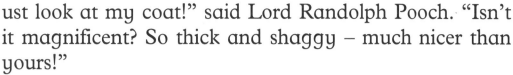
ust look at my coat!" said Lord Randolph Pooch. "Isn't it magnificent? So thick and shaggy – much nicer than yours!"

Randolph was a tiresome puppy – he was so proud of his thick coat – and he could not stop singing its praises to all the other puppies.

But then came summer. . . As June turned to July, and July turned to August, the sun shone brighter and brighter and Randolph became hotter and hotter.

"Isn't this heat unbearable?" said Randolph. "I can't stand it!"

"No, we love it," said his friends. "You're just hot because you're overdressed!"

After that, Randolph kept very quiet about his coat.

Biff Beagle was a remarkable dog. He could do anything. In fact he had done everything. Skateboarding, windsurfing, hang-gliding – you name something adventurous and you can be sure that Biff was a master of it.

The trouble was, this made Biff easily bored. Today was no exception and Biff restlessly paced around the house moping.

"Why don't you go and sail your boat?" said his mother. "That will keep you busy."

"Bored with boats," said Biff.

"What about parachuting?" she suggested.

"Bored with parachuting," said Biff. It was the same with everything.

"Bored! Bored! Bored! Bored!" Biff would say.

"Why don't you read a book then?" asked his mother.

"A book!" said Biff, "What's so adventurous about reading?"

But you know, his mother was right. The book idea was a success. Now Biff was *never* bored. And there were so many books to choose from that he never ran out of adventures! You see books can be very exciting!

The Husky puppies loved the snow. However, one night the snow fell very deep, far deeper than it had fallen for many years. As soon as the sun was up, the Husky puppies rushed out to play, but before they realized what was happening the smallest puppy had sunk deep into a snowdrift. He could not struggle out and no one could see where he was.

It was all very worrying until Growler, the oldest puppy, remembered old Mr. St. Bernard, who lived in the corner cottage.

"I have heard Grandpa saying that in the old days Mr. St. Bernard used to rescue puppies who were lost in the snow," said Growler.

They banged at Mr. St. Bernard's door and told him what had happened.

"Leave everything to me," he woofed. Then he strapped a little barrel of warm milk round his neck and sniffed through the snow until he found the lost puppy. He gave him a drink of milk and carried him home on his shoulders.

"We old dogs always know a few good tricks," smiled Mr. St. Bernard.

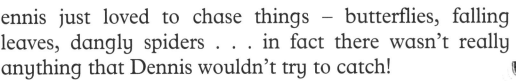

Dennis just loved to chase things – butterflies, falling leaves, dangly spiders . . . in fact there wasn't really anything that Dennis wouldn't try to catch!

"Maybe we should call you 'Buzzy,'" laughed his friends. "You're always buzzing around like a busy bee!"

One day, Dennis caught sight of something out of the corner of his eye; something just behind him, something black and white and moving fast. Slowly, he got ready to pounce . . . then JUMP. He leapt around as fast as lightning. But Dennis wasn't quite fast enough. Whatever it was, was still just behind him. Again he jumped, and again the thing was faster still. Around and around Dennis whizzed, trying to catch the thing, until he collapsed, quite worn out.

"You silly billy," laughed his friends. "You've been chasing your own tail! I think we'd better call you 'Dizzy Dennis' in future."

After that Dennis always thought hard before he chased anything.

I t's your birthday," said Rebecca Redsetter to her mother. "Rosie and I are going to prepare you a special birthday lunch." Saying this, she and her little sister ran downstairs to the kitchen.

"What do grown-ups like to eat?" asked Rosie.

"Well," said Rebecca. "I think they like all the things they want us to eat. Like cabbage and carrots and green beans."

"Yuck!" said Rosie.

Rebecca got all the vegetables out of the cupboard and put them in a big bowl. She put the bowl in the microwave and carefully set the timer – just as Mommy had shown her.

"What shall we have to eat?" asked Rosie.

"It's a celebration so we should have all the things we like to eat," said Rebecca.

Mrs. Redsetter came down to lunch, to be presented with a large plate of overcooked vegetables. "Thank you very much," she said politely, and settled down to eat.

Her birthday *was* slightly ruined by having to watch Rebecca and Rosie eating potato chips, ice cream and chocolate cookies!

Toby sniffed cautiously at the tiny green stone at the side of the garden pond.

"What an unusual looking stone," he said to no one in particular. "Such strange markings. It looks as though it has eyes drawn on either side." He tipped his head to one side and touched the stone with his nose.

He jumped back in surprise! Surely the thing that looked like an eye had blinked at him. Or could it just be that he had blinked himself? He moved back and stared hard. The stone would not outwit him this time. He looked and looked, determined not to blink.

Just when he thought he couldn't keep his eyes from blinking a second longer, the stone eye blinked again.

"You blinked! You blinked! Are you a magic stone? Will you give me three wishes?" barked Toby.

"Don't stare! Don't stare! Are you a fierce monster? Will you eat me for dinner?" croaked the stone at the same moment.

Both said nothing. Then they burst out laughing.

"I'm just a little puppy!" said Toby.

"*I'm* just a little frog!" said the "stone" at the same time. And after such an unusual meeting, they just had to become the best of little friends.

Phyllis Poodle was pretty, it was said. But she was obsessed with how she looked, and spent many hours in front of the mirror admiring herself. In fact, Phyllis had a mirror on every wall, in every room, so that she could look at herself wherever she was and whatever she was doing.

"Oh Phyllis," she cooed one day. "You really are the prettiest little dog I have ever seen."

"Have you seen how stunning I am looking today?" she asked her brother Philip. He smiled politely, but inside he was fed up with his sister's vanity.

"She needs bringing down a peg or two," he muttered. "She spends too long admiring herself and I'm always late for school because she spends so long getting ready." Philip had an idea. Carefully, while Phyllis was asleep, he painted one little red dot on every mirror.

"Aaagh!" screeched Phyllis when she awoke and looked at herself in the mirror. "It can't be true! I've got a spot on my face!"

And do you know? Phyllis spends less time in front of the mirror now. She can't bear to see that spot.

What am I going to give Uncle Humphrey for his birthday?" wondered Sophie. "I've hardly got any pocket money, and Uncle Humphrey doesn't seem to need anything."

Sophie was right. Sir Humphrey Basset-Hound was a dog who lacked nothing. He had everything: a beautiful house, a shiny sports car, expertly groomed hair, a well-combed moustache, a very smart suit and even a solid silver monocle in his right eye.

"I know. I'll give him my favorite yellow ribbon," thought Sophie. "It didn't cost me much but I love it – I do hope Uncle Humph does too."

Sophie's ribbon was Uncle Humphrey's favorite present. "I can tie it to my monocle, which keeps falling off. And it matches my suit! What a brilliant idea!" said Humphrey.

Jack planted the seed carefully in the pot. He watered it every day, never forgetting, and never letting it get soggy. This was an important seed and he wanted it to grow into a tall, strong plant. Jack might even be able to climb up it! Grandpa did say it would grow into a beanstalk, just like in the story.

After what seemed a dreadfully long time, the earth began to rise up in a little bump in the pot. Then Jack noticed a speck of white, then more and more, until the tiny stem arched out of the dark earth and two leaves spread out as though stretching after a long sleep.

Soon it was time to plant it in the garden. Jack found a patch of earth and dug a little hole. Gently he popped the plant in the hole, filled it with soft earth and patted it down.

Every day he watched it. Every day he watered it. Every day it grew a little taller until it was up to his knees . . . then his waist . . . then his chest . . . then way above his head. Lovely red flowers came next and finally, to Jack's delight, the beans!

"It won't grow up to the clouds!" laughed Grandpa. "But you do have your very own beanstalk and there's no danger of a giant chasing you around."

The new house was almost finished. Martin the handyman was just painting the living room walls in a lovely deep red. Everybody was pleased with it.

The only member of the Chihuahua family who wasn't happy with the new house was Sam. Ever since they'd moved in Sam had felt neglected. Everyone was so busy with the decorating and furnishing that Sam was left to play on his own. And Sam didn't like this at all. He wandered from room to room, wanting attention from somebody. But Mom was sorting out the play-room, Dad was putting up shelves in the kitchen, and even his sister Sandra was helping out by making curtains.

"I know," he thought. "Martin will play with me." And he bounded through to the living room. But no one was there. In the middle of the newly-decorated room, stood a great big ladder, some paintbrushes, and a large can of red paint. But Sam didn't notice the paint. He was too busy feeling sorry for himself and he walked right into the ladder, knocking over the paint. The paint poured across the polished, wooden floor. Sam panicked and scampered quickly out of the door, across the hall, up the stairs and all the way up to his bedroom to hide.

What Sam didn't realize was that he'd left a bright trail of red footprints behind him. He was sure to get plenty of attention now!

When the big puppies were at school, Mommy Afghan took Baby for a quiet swing and some sand pie making in the playground.

During the school vacation all the puppies went to the playground together. Baby had to wait for a turn on the swings and when he did get on, his brothers pushed him far higher than Mommy ever did. Right up to the sky he whizzed and then came swooshing down again. After that it was into the sandpit to make sand pies by the dozen and stamp all over them as fast as they were made. When Mommy wasn't looking the big puppies even put sand down each other's backs and squealed and wriggled. It was exciting and the afternoon flew by as if it were only a few seconds long. Baby loved it – in a way, but when the vacation was over, he was glad to get back to the quiet times with Mommy.

"Life's like that," explained Mommy. "Without gentle days there are no thrilling adventurous times."

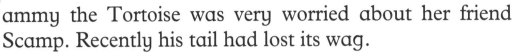

Tammy the Tortoise was very worried about her friend Scamp. Recently his tail had lost its wag.

"I know. I'll cheer him up," she said to herself. So she offered Scamp some delicious chocolate cookies. But Scamp said, "You haven't got any ginger cookies have you?" and wandered off.

The next day Tammy decided to try again, "Come for a walk with me," she said. Scamp trotted beside her for a bit then said, "Can you walk any faster?" Of course Tammy couldn't so Scamp ran off, his tail drooping behind him.

By now Tammy was really worried. Perhaps Scamp had forgotten how to wag his tail. So Tammy said, "Scamp. I'm going to show you how to get your wag back. Pretend my head is your tail." Then Tammy began to shake her head slowly from left to right. It was the slowest, silliest, strangest pretend tail Scamp had ever seen.

In fact it was so funny Scamp couldn't help laughing and pretty soon his tail wagged so hard it almost dropped off!

Harold was a mischievous pup and if you couldn't find him standing outside the classroom, as a punishment, then he was probably in the library learning woof-poetry by heart because he'd played one too many tricks that day.

"What trouble did he cause?" you ask.

Well . . . he glued down desk lids, he stuck chewing gum to the teachers' chairs, he howled off key in assembly . . . and the list goes on. One Friday the head teacher announced that a new art teacher was arriving; "His name is Mr. Brushe." Harold giggled. "I want *all* of you to behave for him," and at this point he glared at Harold.

Harold trotted off home and spent the whole weekend planning new and naughty tricks. By Monday the class sat giggling, waiting for the new teacher to fall into Harold's trap.

In he strode at 9:00 AM – ducking to one side and neatly avoiding the bucket of water which had been positioned to fall on him.

Turning around he said, "I should warn you, I was once the class-prankster and I know every trick in the puppy joke book."

Harold behaved unusually well after that.

For Mr. Brushe at least.

I'm busy," said Grandpa, "so don't bother me. I've put a pirate ship in the garden for you to sail across the sea in and find the treasure. Take this," he added, and gave them a grubby roll of paper tied with a red ribbon.

The two puppies raised their eyebrows, but they were both curious. They unrolled the paper, which crackled slightly in their hands as though it was ancient. Spreading it out they gasped. It was a very old map – a treasure map, covered with mysterious signs, just itching to be unraveled!

"Come on, Cap'n, let's hoist the mainsail, splice the main brace and set off to Timbuktu!" shouted Patrick. (It sounded like the right thing to say.)

Some time later, the two puppies sat breathless and grubby, recounting their adventure.

". . . and then the seas crashed around us as our ship made her way through the storms. The waves grew so high we were washed overboard."

"The next thing I remember, I was lying on a beautiful beach."

"Yes, and I had the map clenched in my fist. So we searched the island, escaped from the wild animals, found the treasure, built a new boat and sailed all the way back and . . ."

". . . All that just in time for dinner!" laughed Grandpa.